THE Second Child

RANDOM HOUSE NEW YORK

THE Second Child

poems

Deborah Garrison

Published in the United States by Random House, an imprint of The Random
House Publishing Group, a division of Random House, Inc., New York.

RANDOM HOUSE and colophon are registered trademarks of Random House, Inc.

Some of the poems in this work were originally published
in *The New Yorker* and *The Yale Review.*

LIBRARY OF CONGRESS CATALOGING-IN-PUBLICATION DATA
Garrison, Deborah.
The second child: poems / Deborah Garrison.
p.   cm.
ISBN 978-1-4000-6359-8
1. Motherhood—Poetry.   I. Title.
PS3557.A734S43 2007
811'.54—dc22   2006040631

Printed in the United States of America on acid-free paper
www.atrandom.com
2   4   6   8   9   7   5   3

Designed by Stephanie Huntwork

NOW DO U UNDERSTAND WHAT HEAVEN IS   IT IS THE SURROUND OF THE LIVING

—James Merrill, *The Changing Light at Sandover*

1

2

1

On New Terms

I'd like to begin again. Not touch my
own face, not tremble in the dark before
an intruder who never arrives. Not
apologize. Not scurry, not pace. Not
refuse to keep notes of what meant the most.
Not skirt my father's ghost. Not abandon
piano, or a book before the end.
Not count, count, count and wait, poised—the control,
the agony controlled—for the loss of
the one, having borne, I can't be, won't breathe
without: the foregone conclusion, the pain
not yet met, the preemptive mourning
without which

        nothing left of me but smoke.

Goodbye, New York
(song from the wrong side of the Hudson)

You were the big fat city we called hometown
You were the lyrics I sang but never wrote down

You were the lively graves by the highway in Queens
the bodega where I bought black beans

stacks of the *Times* we never read
nights we never went to bed

the radio jazz, the doughnut cart
the dogs off their leashes in Tompkins Square Park

You were the tiny brass mailbox key
the joy of "us" and the sorrow of "me"

You were the balcony bar in Grand Central Station
the blunt commuters and their destination

the post-wedding blintzes at 4 A.M.
and the pregnant waitress we never saw again

You were the pickles, you were the jar
You were the prizefight we watched in a bar

the sloppy kiss in the basement at Nell's
the occasional truth that the fortune cookie tells

Sinatra still swinging at Radio City
You were ugly and gorgeous but never pretty

always the question, never the answer
the difficult poet, the aging dancer

the call I made from a corner phone
to a friend in need, who wasn't at home

the fireworks we watched from a tenement roof
the brash allegations and the lack of any proof

my skyline, my byline, my buzzer and door
now you're the dream we lived before

Not Pleasant but True

This afternoon when the bus turned
hard by the graveyard,

the stones sugared with snow,
I wanted to go there, underground.

You're thirteen weeks old.
Cold shock, as never wished before:

to die and be buried, close
under the packed earth,

safe for an eternal instant
from my constant, fevered fear that

you'd die. Relief
warming my veins,

and you relieved forever
of my looming, teary watch.

Someone take from me
this crazed love,

such battering care
I lost my mind—

I was going to leave you
without a mother!

Play Your Hand

A joy so full it won't fit
in a body. Like sound packed
in a trumpet's bell, its glossy
exit retains that shape, printing

its curve in reverse on the ear.
A musical house, with more
children than you planned for,
a smallest hand, and fingers

of that hand closing on one
of yours, making a handle,
pulling the lever gaily
down, ringing in the first

jackpot of many, with coins
and cries, heavenly noise,
a crashing pile
of minor riches—

And if the worst thing imaginable
were to happen
where does the happiness
go?

The melody flown
(where?), you think you wouldn't
live one more day.
But you would.

Days don't stop.
You toss your glove at the moon,
you don't know what
may come down.

Both Square and Round

You moments I court—

Back of the head settled
in arm's crook,
rump in my palm,
the whole half a body
just the length of my forearm,
small face twitching toward
repose. From the window
lamplight or moonlight slides
on the creamy forehead,
the new-bulb smoothness
at the temples both squared
and rounding, the flickering play
of shapes suggesting, mysteriously,
intelligence within.
And the triangular
center peak, V-bottom
of a heart where pure skin
shades into the gold dusting
of first hair, nearly

fur, like halo's fuzz,
more light than matter—

What was it, just
then, I swore to myself
I'd keep?

As though I could hold
a magnifying glass
to time

and slow its shaping
us.

A Short Skirt on Broadway

See that girl?
See that quick
no-nonsense
joying in itself
walk?
Soft scissoring,
slight hitch where
the blades meet,
then flash apart,
re-meet?

Just so I
used to walk.
I used to have
"legs." The small
trill in the gait
like a half smile,
tossed free at those who'd look.
Self-ish pleasure on my walk

downtown with nowhere
in mind to go

was the best kind
before I found another so
ordinary I wasn't going to
mention it. Have you
ever been in the shuttered room
where life is milk? Where you make
milk? And by a series of peppery
tugs, urgent frothings, symphonic arcing
spurts (how absurd, how bovine)
you leave yourself aside
for someone else?
I was milk.
She was milk.
Even *he* was milk.

Now when I hurry across
Times Square, pants-suited,
no one sees me. And I'm not
walking in the city—that old simplicity
I've learned not to miss, not much—

but getting out
of it, westbound,
to feed her dinner.
I wish the milk had lasted longer,
but she got legs of her own.

The Past Is Still There

I've forgotten so much.
What it felt like back then,
what we said to each other.

But sometimes when I'm standing
at the kitchen counter after dinner
and I look out the window at the dark

thinking of nothing,
something swims up.
Tonight this:

your laughing into my mouth
as you were trying
to kiss me.

How Many

How tall is this house?
How many stories,
how many can I stack
and how high?
How many windows, bunks,
baskets, spoonfuls,
jars and towels,
pillows and bowls,
night lights will we keep?

How many revolutions down this hill
will a body tumble,
flattening how many
grasses?
How many blades
carpet the way
as galaxies do sky,
and how many stars, when bodies
lie still, can eyes spy?

How many years can each
in her turn outlast my wishes?

How many, exactly?

For I want more—
yet more
voices that pierce
my heart utterly.

Bedtime Story

Number Two happy at the tit
in the nursery while First One has a bit

of truck with Dad
on the big bed

in our room. A chin
of whiskers on a clean

belly, a question posed:
Daddy, what are those

lines on your face? Oh,
they're just because I'm getting old. . . .

I hear it coming, Two all unsuspecting
in the in-breathing, jaw-working, lactating

trance, as One: *You mean, you're dying?*
He: *What? I'm diving?*

And she: *No DYING,* insisting, *When*
you're old is when

you die!
For didn't I

tell her—I did!—that Granddad
died from being old?

I almost hear his
mind race, the soundless

shift to *No no! Not*
old like that!

And the cascading (as Two snorts,
pops off to burp) forth

of explanations (not enough),
confirmation (sure enough)

of One's new fear:
When you die, it's like, you disappear?

Had him there.
Yes disappear. No longer here.

A brief silence (the suck subsides,
Two lolls and sighs)

till One, awail against
the sight of it,

tall door closing on us
all, blurts tremulous:

I don't WANT to disappear!
And he: *There, there . . .*

Weeping with her now
as I put Two down,

safe crib, sweet ignorance,
thumb plugged against the chance

squall, the first knowledge
that is anguish,

and I tuck my empty
breast away

weeping and muttering, *Laid*
to rest, she's laid

to rest, she'll lay me to rest
they'll lay us to rest.

I Saw You Walking

I saw you walking in Newark Penn Station
in your shoes of white ash. At the corner
of my nervous glance your dazed passage
first forced me away, tracing the crescent
berth you'd give a drunk, a lurcher, nuzzling
all comers with ill will and his stench, but
not this one, not today: one shirt arm's sheared
clean from the shoulder, the whole bare limb
wet with muscle and shining dimly pink,
the other full-sheathed in cotton, Brooks Bros.
type, the cuff yet buttoned at the wrist, a
parody of careful dress, preparedness—
so you had not rolled up your sleeves yet this
morning when your suit jacket (here are
the pants, dark gray, with subtle stripe, as worn
by men like you on ordinary days)
and briefcase (you've none, reverse commuter
come from the pit with nothing to carry
but your life) were torn from you, as your life
was not. Your face itself seemed to be walking,
leading your body north, though the age

of the face, blank and ashen, passing forth
and away from me, was unclear, the sandy
crown of hair powdered white like your feet, but
underneath not yet gray—forty-seven?
forty-eight? the age of someone's father—
and I trembled for your luck, for your broad
dusted back, half shirted, walking away;
I should have dropped to my knees to thank God
you were alive, O my God, in whom I don't believe.

.

2

The Second Child

You see I too
was second in order. Two.

Before you arrived
for a time I cried

nightly at the fattening, spelling the end
of our tight, well-tended

trio. The carefully scheduled bliss
of bath and bed—luxurious

brace of both to read a single book,
darting between us, her drinking-all-in, wee weighty look,

her finger-gesture toward some new developmental toy
or crystal bit of babble our post-crib nightcap, rehashed joy . . .

Now no rehash, littler miss,
of your airy imitation of her searing kiss:

down babyhood's brief corridor you disappear behind
her, the master dancer, your tutor in body and mind;

you not just child but sister. And while
she—so fierce, perversely proud—will be not child

but childhood's star, and pound the trail
and suffer in her art and, hell or high, refuse to fail

(you see it hurts, I love her so),
you will carelessly, sly, my sidelong darling, go

after: first toddling understudy, then patiently aslant
toward something other, invited by a glint I can't

discount. When your delighted eyes
dance at her back, assess the scene, I surmise

the end, and your means
to it. Like me—

for now I see, you showed me—
you'll be happy.

"Mother, may I inherit your grace"

(at Michiana)

Mother, may I inherit your grace
while you're still around to enjoy it—
may I grasp your secret genus, your type,
be it birch, tall and knot-freckled, ghost-lighting
the darker unnamed trees on our walk, or,
as in your fortieth spring, new widow,
greenest willow bending low? So low,
but flexible; carrying multiple currents
suddenly in multiple arms.
Maybe you're one of the dangling opals,
long-stemmed, gold-edged—your engagement
present, passed on for mine; luminescent,
of mixed colors, you flower in the dark. . . .
Or, more comically, are you cousin
to the cat your sister let drop from the fire escape,
Chicago 1948 it would be, to prove to the boys
he'd land on his feet? He did, though broke
two legs. A survival you told of repeatedly.

I wonder how I'd do as you,
drifting behind you to the lake tonight.
I see my stride matching yours,
my arms swinging in time, hips the same
width. Our thoughts double as we glance
south along the bend toward Indiana:
that shore where you, half naked, Peter-Panned
as a girl, crisp on the rippling dune,
the crescent of fresh-hammered shanties
kibitzing under stars.
Those Friday nights, sundown at nine,
the fathers arrived with provisions; you bathed in the lake.
Now nothing of tree or sand
or the much-painted dream to be seen.
It's all a steel mill.
You turn and smile at your daughter
coming along. No offense to the memory,
but you, now and ever, prefer the present.

A Drink in the Night

My eyes opened
at once for you were standing
by my side, you'd padded
in to ask for a drink in the night.

The cup was—where?
Fallen down, behind?
Churning in the dishwasher, downstairs?
Too tired to care, I cupped
my hand and tipped it
to you. You stared, gulped,
some cold down your chin.
Whispered, "Again!"

O wonder. You'd no idea
I could make a cup.
You've no idea what
I can do for you, or hope to.
You watched, curious and cool,

as I cupped some up
to my own lips, too,
then asked,
"Why does it taste *better*?"

Poem About an Owl

I've never seen an owl
Not a real one

But often enough at night
Have started up at the wingbeat:

Long, with loaded silence between lengths
Like velvet ripping

The children's-book eyes
Saucerish and startled with wisdom

Sweeping the forest floor
For a little something, a little something

And I leapt from sleep
If indeed I was sleeping

Belted my robe like a mother of old
And rushed to their beds to see

If it got them, the skidding talon,
Where they were quietly

Breathing in their own
Animal dreams

A Human Calculation

If it had to be him
or them
let it be him.

If he had to choose between me
and them,
just one of them,
goodbye to me.

Take me,
take him,
God forbid them.

Blasphemous
back of the envelope:
we don't get
to subtract
or make trades.
Only to add
and clutch
at our number.

Sestina for
the Working Mother

No time for a sestina for the working mother.
Who has so much to do, from first thing in the morning
When she has to get herself dressed and the children
Too, when they tumble in the pillow pile rather than listening
To her exhortations about brushing teeth, making ready for the day;
They clamor with "up" hugs when she struggles out the door.

Every time, as if shot from a cannon when she shuts the door.
She stomps down the street in her city boots, slipping from mother
Mode into commuter trance, trees swaying at the corner of a new day
Nearly turned, her familiar bus stop cool and welcoming in the morning.
She hears her own heart here, though no one else is listening,
And if the bus is late she hears down the block the voices of her children

Bobbing under their oversized backpacks to greet other children
At their own bus stop. They too have come flying from the door,
Brave for the journey, and everyone is talking and no one is listening
As they head off to school. The noisy children of the working mother,
Waiting with their sitter for the bus, are healthy and happy this morning,
And that's the best way, the mother knows, for a day

To begin. The apprehension of what kind of day
It will be in the world of work, blissful without children,
Trembles in the anxious and pleasurable pulse of the morning;
It has tamped her down tight and lit her out the door
And away from what she might have been as a mother
At home, perhaps drinking coffee and listening

To NPR, what rapt and intelligent listening
She'd do at home. And volunteering, she thinks, for part of the day
At their school—she'd be a playground monitor, a PTA mother!
She'd see them straggle into the sunshine, her children
Bright in the slipstream, and she a gracious shadow at the school door;
She would not be separated from them for long by the morning.

But she has chosen her flight from them, on this and every morning.
She's now so far away she trusts someone else is listening
To their raised voices, applying a Band-Aid, opening the door
For them when the sunshine calls them out into the day.
At certain moments, head bent at her desk, she can see her children,
And feels a quick stab. She hasn't forgotten that she is their mother.

Every weekday morning, every working day,
She listens to her heart and the voices of her children.
Goodbye! they shout, and the door closes behind the working mother.

To the Man in a Loden Coat

Hey, mister,
man in a loden coat
standing in front of me
on the escalator and blocking my
way—
I know
I'm self-absorbed,
particularly at this hour,
5:22 to be precise and I need
to make the 5:25 home—
don't you know that in this city,
in this life, we
walk on the left,
stand on the right?

Don't tell me to chill out,
don't tell me to "breathe,"
I hate breathing,
I mean unless it is happening
without my knowing it,
which is, thank God, most of the time,

and don't tell me life is long
because it actually isn't;
it's all I can do not to
give you a sweet shove
on your long loden back,
same as all the bottled-up
left-lane travelers
behind *me* want to do
to my navy-clad shoulder,
a nice blue to your green,
like water for the earth,
sky for the forest,
green and blue a tea for two,
etc., among the vistas
that call me home now,
at 5:23, about to miss the bus,
so would you please

MOVE OVER?

Either Way, No Way

The consuming obsession:
When it will come. When, next,
Will they come?

Not when you're counting your blessings
Or planning your future
But when you're combing your hair or dialing the phone
Or remembering the number in the moment
Just before dialing the phone

Not when you're waving from the deck
A tearful goodbye, regretting the trip,
But earlier, when you're packing the trunk,
Folding clothes absently
And wondering which shoes you'll wear

Not when you're scanning the crowd
Alert and aware
But when you're buying ice cream
Or chatting with the man
Who sells the ice cream

Who came here from Greece
When he was only sixteen
To make a new life

Not when you're afraid
But when you're not afraid

Not at the graduation, the convention or ball
Not when the hall is full
But when it's all over and you in your suit
Are handing your stub
To the parking attendant
Or dropping your keys on the table
Unknotting your tie, humming the night's melody

Not when you're watching history unfold on TV
But when you're reaching for milk
In the clutter of the fridge or putting cold packs
In lunches or braiding their hair
Or driving them there,

And you note pulling out of the driveway
The newspaper still sheathed in plastic
On the lawn, which is a bit overlong
And polished with dew—a lovely sight,

Fresh morn for the eye
Which formerly
You might have looked through
Without seeing

And by the way
That was no way
To live either.

Pink and White

Peonies are the only flower I care for
and when I saw them from the window
yesterday, tumbled and heavy along
a fence, fully exploded, nodding
at the ground, hanging their heads but not
yet spoiled, I remembered
a summer (maybe seven years
ago, or was it ten?) I wasn't sure
our love would come again,
and here I am, almost

kissing the grass like that,
bursting and rich, cracked
all over like broken cake—
makes you cry but still sweet.

September Poem

Now can I say?
On that blackest day,

When I learned of
The uncountable, the hell-bent obscenity,

I felt, with shame, a seed in me,
Powerful and inarticulate:

I wanted to be pregnant.
Women in the street flowing toward

Home, dazed with grief, and my daze
Admixed with jealous awe, I wondered

If they were,
Or wished for it, too,

To be full, to be forming,
To be giving our blood's food

To the yet to be.
To feel the warp of morning's

Hormonal chucking, the stutter kiss
Of first movement. At first,

The idea of sex a further horror:
To take pleasure in a collision

Of bodies was vile, self-centered, too lush.
But the pushy, ennobling pulse

Of the ordinary won't halt
For good taste. Or knows nothing of tragedy.

Thus. Today I have a boy
A week old. Blessed surplus:

A third child.
Have you heard mothers,

Matter-of-fact, call the third
The insurance policy?

That wasn't why.
And not because when so many people

Die we want, crudely pining,
To replace them with more people.

But for the wild, heaven-grazing
Pleasure and pain of the arrival.

The small head crushed and melony
After a journey

Out. Sheer cliff
Of the first day, flat in bed, gut-empty,

Ringed by memories and sharp cries.
Sharp bliss in proximity to the roundness,

The globe already set aspin, particular,
Of a whole new life.

Which might in any case
End in towering sorrow.

3

Birth Day Pun

My body wants to make a joke,
is gathering itself up
in spasms as for
a sneeze.
But a sneeze,
a long hard cackle,
of the whole body.

They say when you need
to sneeze, look at the light

and I do, and I feel
a brilliance inside, cutting me
with its million rays. What's this?
A flaming ring that expands
and tightens in my gut,
hungry and burning its way
down to the butt of my self—

A smoldering butt!
That's how it is:

suddenly here,
the down-bearing pressure,
the familiar prehistoric wailing
wish to shit it out . . .

and someone in the room
is screaming,
comically, like a parody of a woman,
Why? Why does it
hurt SO much?

as the ring of fire
in a gaseous flowering
rips through and leaves me seared.

At once I understand
that was me screaming and hear
the doctor, from beyond the thrumming bounds
of self and sense: "You have a sun."

What?
A sun?
Then I get it!
I made a pun.

I want to crow and cup
the steaming, tender parts

that make him son.

Unbidden Sonnet
with Evergreen

Round midnight we were drifting cheek to cheek
and you in sighing rhythmic beats pulled down
your milk; please, siphon off a bit of life—
what's mine is yours—and grow; you grow so you
can go from me, I know, yet I drink in
the sweet increase that will divide us.
The hand that kneads my breast, bell-pulls my hair,
is chubbier, more chubby as I stare,
and in the window stands the churchyard pine,
whose needled song must pierce through mine: *he may*
grow tall yet I'll be taller still than ten
of him, and year on year I'll stand in rain
and sun, still sentry here when he is gone—
The rosebud grip is loosed, the feeding's done.

Song After Everyone's Asleep

When I woke in the night with a mania
to please you and shifted so you'd shift and
half-wake too, in the dark without my glasses, you
without yours, I reached into your shorts; your lashes
flicked up, and in the blur I caught the smoother face
of the boy you were when you first grabbed my hand
on the path through the woods behind the school yard,
a stone's throw from my mother's house—
when I felt suddenly entire, that I was a whole body
holding another whole body with my hand.

We can never go back there.
But with eyes still closed you smile
permission for me, with my hand,
to keep you awake awhile.

A Midnight Bris

You, my doctor, my captain,
my adviser and examiner,
came in your civvies,
your jeans and black shirt,
from a show and late supper with your wife
to circumcise the baby.
Carrying a small jar of red wine from dinner—
I'd soon see what for.
I was waiting up, old-timer in my
sweats and clean socks on the hospital bed,
because you'd promised,
after our long run,
to do this yourself.

"You sure you want to come?
You can wait here and I'll tell you it's done."
No, I would go. I would see.
Into the nighttime nursery where you swiftly
strapped him to a board, a tiny torture,
performed without apology or fear
of my fear. Suddenly there was none.

Quivering boy, the face all nose,
eyes mostly closed; I stood by
with my hand on his damp
head, stilled and curious.
I was a Jew after all, as were they—
my atheist father who wept when I found
moldy postcards from Poland in the basement,
my mother whose grandparents were socialists.
Your great-great-grandfather went back to Russia
to design the Moscow subway, I beamed
to the baby as the doctor got the knife ready
and clamped the penis expertly;
his daughter, my mother's red-haired mother,
danced on the Yiddish stage in Chicago. . . .

The doctor was Jewish too,
rabbinical with his black beard
and his reverent study of weeks and days,
the surplus intelligence of those
who live by the love their hands deliver.
How many times he'd grasped
and held my cervix, and me in thrall—
how many jokes and tales, whistling
"La Vie en Rose" when I pushed out the first.
There wasn't much crying after all,

and no blood to speak of. The pacifier dipped in wine
as he instructed, the baby sucked and was calmed.

Back in my room, I sat alert
as he took the clipboard to sign my release
for the morning. My last time.
He looked up and I stared at the tears in his eyes.
"But you . . . so many patients . . ."
"They're not all the same," he said.
We let that stand.
It was like everything else here, in delivery's twilight:
the pure grief and triumph gone too soon,
there would be nothing like it
the rest of your life.
He didn't say, "You could have one more."
"I wish . . ." I began.
But I couldn't.
He kissed my cheek and said, "You did good."

The Necklace

He lay idling along me,
one leg crossed at the other knee, jauntily,

tiny man at his dinner, when
with brio sucked me in and wah-wahed

his jaw in quasi parody of his quest—
drinking but playing at drinking,

rhyming his eye with mine
and his was full of laughter as his starfish hand

upstretched, twirling to conduct the air,
to turn a song from nothing, waved

high and snagged of a sudden
the slender chain, platinum whisper

at my neck (dangled from which,
a diamond his father gave when *she* was born):

He couldn't care!
Just tugging there—by accident,

or in a freshman stumble toward
intent?—was for him a joyous

purpose, a study of texture,
of that solid link that might resist

his pull,
or not.

It took me a long minute
to unpeel that clutching paw,

and by the way it felt all wrong,
against nature.

See, if left to my own I'd let him
grasp without a thought

what was mine
and break it.

Into the Lincoln Tunnel

The bus rolled into the Lincoln Tunnel,
and I was whispering a prayer
that it not be today, not today, please
no shenanigans, no blasts, no terrors,
just please the rocking, slightly nauseating
gray ride, stop and start, chug-a
in the dim fellowship of smaller cars,
bumper lights flickering hello and warning.
Yes, please smile upon these good
people who want to enter the city and work.
Because work is good, actually, and life is good,
despite everything, and I don't mean to sound
spoiled, but please don't think I don't know
how grateful I should be
for what I do have—

I wonder whom I'm praying to.
Maybe Honest Abe himself,
craggy and splendid in his tall chair,
better than God to a kid;
Lincoln whose birthday I shared,

in whom I took secret pride: born, thus I was,
to be truthful, and love freedom.

Now with a silent collective sigh
steaming out into the broken winter sun,
up the ramp to greet buildings, blue brick
and brown stone and steel, candy-corn pylons
and curving guardrails massively bolted and men
in hard hats leaning on resting machines
with paper cups of coffee—

a cup of coffee, a modest thing to ask
Abe for,
dark, bitter, fresh
as an ordinary morning.

Dad, You Returned
to Me Again

The transparent clarity
of childhood happiness,
like water.

That colorless sparkling,
tasteless but so fresh.
To drink, or ribboning over
a large stone along the brambled
bank of a river I remember.
Said to be a large wily brown
trout under there.

Two children astride me
in rumpled bed this A.M.,
and when she petted
his baby head, crooning a word
almost his name,
his eyes hooked her face,
his hands discovered applause
in halting pace:

clap (pause) clap clap!
Their mingled laughter,
the nickname,
the merry clap-clap,
the jerking bright giggles

so free I dropped through time
and saw again the iridescence
across the belly of a trout
slipping whole in my hand
in sunlight for just long enough
to see not the usual liverish
speckling of brown but the spray
of pink, pale blue, gold-yellow
you said meant
"Rainbow,"
and I grasped him, wet and muscular,
smuggled in our air
for a wild moment before your
expert hand unhooked
and slipped him back.

A Joke

Drinking on my left tonight
you tossed up your left
hand and sweetly poked
your index finger in my mouth,
and I, amusing myself, sucked it
in time with you—you all
mine, good enough to eat,
blank baby boychik.

But oh! Your eyes filled up with
mirth, your brows flew up,
you tossed back a hail
of startling bullet notes
and then to make the joke
again, clamped mouth back on
and pushed the finger farther
in, chop chop! Inviting me
with milktime beat.

I didn't laugh along.
The joke, containing as it must

a stab at language——*I suckee,*
you suckee, we suckee!——
branded you a sophisticate
beyond babyhood. There came
a shudder at the teasing, near-
sexual premise, not felt with girls,
and the tears, pressing up
at the punch line:
Goodbye, good boy.

What love, what sorrow,
to give you the heave-ho:
I'll have to wean you
starting tomorrow.

Add One

She's five.
Wants to know
What infinity is.

I try: you take the biggest
Number, you think the last
Number there is, and you add
One more.
See?
You can always add one.
So then the number's
Bigger still.
Infinity means—
The numbers go on
Forever.

She thinks. Index finger raised.
Swiveling innocently Elvis-style
Hips in her big-girl jeans
And shaking her pigtails

In a trance of musing. Then
Cocks her head, terrier-set:

"Is it like, God is still
Alive, making numbers?"

Now, who told her—it wasn't me!—
That God and infinity
Are spoken in one breath?
That what's infinite
Must be divine?

Who, I ask you?

Cascade

The thing about a love poem is
I don't know what to thank you for.
Which or when.
Taxis hissing in the rain,
a million moments, the hotel in Paris

where we laughed because it was so odd
we happened to be us (of all the gin joints . . .),
stripping each other
on Thanksgiving afternoon
across the ocean from ourselves.

The iron bedstead from the farmhouse
in Elyria, house of your aunt Agnes I never met,
but can see like yesterday her clouded, ancient face
greeting you at the door (you were ten, in jeans):
"I always liked a man in uniform."

Newspapers in the bathtub.
Geese to terrify you patrolling the yard.
See, I can almost
remember your memories—
almost. Well the bed frame

wasn't quite wide enough
even for a double so the mattress
stuck out the sides. The head end's curving
top bar had a precise dent we joked about.
And there in the east-facing bedroom on 4th Street,

in sight of our sunlit green copper dome,
our morning water towers
far and near, an unplanned abundance
was modeling itself around us.
In that bed we could learn to make children.

We did have to learn, even sex,
we were that young. And once
when I cried—isn't it strange,
I don't remember about what—
you held my hand,

held me a long time
as we lay there
so I could revisit some old pain,
feel it shifting in your regard
to become a silvered third shape

between us, an upstart,
bright cascade of energy
I could perhaps keep.
I still have it.
I could thank you for that.

Someday We Will Have to Drop the Objects to Which Our Hands Now Cling

Just as, seal-style, belly first,
the baby flung himself across
the toilet's lid and, gripping its rim,
hoisted self to stand astride as on
the curve of a world, toddler king,
to potchke with delights of the countertop—
prescription pills and razors and tweezers,
anything sharp, spillable, fillable, or liable
to choke him—his sister, three and a half,
toothbrush in mouth, blurted pastily:
"We'll always have Walty, won't we?"
I startled. "Yes! But what do you mean?"
"I mean, he will never die, right? He's too little."

Do I get to lie?
For I agree, he's too little, as is she.
Yes, darling, as you decree,
let it be written:

All ye littlest,
youngest, least tested and tried, so urgent
to climb, in face of hazards—yes, hazards
on all sides is best, so they can learn to fall
and stand, to judge and spurn, to swerve and skirt
all evil, pain, and harm— Let the littlest
be most blessed.

A Piece of Paper

A piece of paper
drifted from the mess on the kitchen table
down to the floor, where it would stay
until I picked it up to throw it away.

Page turned over, a crayoned six-pointed
star blazes there, the work of our second
by its vital, slightly wobbling hand.
She's filled in each of the seven fields

defined when triangles mesh: magenta, mustard,
lawn green, baby blue—the whole slightly
skewed as though the star's leaning to eavesdrop
from on high, or shuffling off to Buffalo, stage left . . .

I hesitate at the trash.
A piece of pure absorption in color and symbol—
such passing mysteries and their products
we don't celebrate or record:

kitchen table after dinner, her silent in a small
bliss of making, forehead nearly touching
the sheet ripped from an older one's homework binder.
A star is more than homework,

and less. But there's so much paper here—
so many of these whimsies, bills,
spelling lists, shopping lists,
soccer schedules, calendars,

even, too soon to toss, a first apology
(GIGI SORY I TOOK YOUR PENGWIN
IF YOU FORGIVE ME
CHEK THE BOX YES OR NO!!)—

the crucial form to be posted's often buried,
the pictures saved but lost.
Never will it all be catalogued,
I know. But how to get a view

from above, to see the long dusty arc
of the continuing itself, the multiplying
of relevant beside irrelevant,
no survival of the fittest

or intelligent design, but a profusion
of stars to flare
and be crumpled,
drawn again another day?

Above the Roar

When I was unhappy
words slipped ceaselessly
from my pen,
arrows down the page,
tears run together,
running to tell.

But when I was happy—
when a second girl
slid out of my body
on the third breath,
glistening with the caul
still on her head
(like Caesar, the doctor said);
when she clamped onto me
and my uterus buckled and
I was weeping for everything I'd lost
that she couldn't lose
because those things were
already gone;
when her sister was belting

"Daisy, Daisy, give me your answer true!"
up and down the back stairs;
when one or the other
lit with fever lay humped
on my chest and I was burning
another vigil to the flicker
of shallow breathing,
that candle of worry
just the length of one night;
when I looked into your eyes
and heard your mind clearly
and answered silently yes,
I love you, I adore you
(and it was loud, my ears were roaring);
when I chased the baby
down the hall where he dashed,
penis flying, proud and squealing,
to delay his bath a hundreth time—

I was wordless, free . . .

Look at me grab him!

ACKNOWLEDGMENTS

Grateful acknowledgment is made to the publications where
some of these poems previously appeared, and to their editors.

The New Yorker: "Dad, You Returned to Me Again" (as "Dad, You
    Returned to Me This Morning"), "Into the Lincoln Tunnel,"
    "I Saw You Walking," "On New Terms," "Pink and White,"
    "September Poem," "The Second Child."
McSweeneys.net: "Sestina for the Working Mother."
Open City: "Add One," "A Short Skirt on Broadway," "Both
    Square and Round," "The Necklace."
The Yale Review: "The Past Is Still There," "Unbidden Sonnet with
    Evergreen."

ABOUT THE AUTHOR

DEBORAH GARRISON is the author of *A Working Girl Can't Win: And Other Poems.* Born in Ann Arbor, Michigan, she worked on the editorial staff of *The New Yorker* for many years and is now an editor at Alfred A. Knopf and Pantheon Books. She lives with her husband and children in Montclair, New Jersey.

This book is set in Spectrum, a typeface designed in the 1940s, the last from the distinguished Dutch type designer Jan van Krimpen. Spectrum is a polished and reserved font.